Welcome to Year 5 handwriting. Here you'll find earthquakes, avalanches, landslides, tornadoes and other natural disasters.

You've been invited to join the famed International Disaster Rescue Squad. Fill in your ID card below.

IDRS

INTERNATIONAL DISASTER RESCUE SQUAD

Name: ______________________

____

Date of birth: ______________________

Residence: ______________________

____

Years of training: ______________________

Disaster-fighting experience: ______________________

____

____

____

Most memorable rescue: ______________________

____

____

____

Motto: ______________________

____

Date __/__/__

Copy this text into the lines below. Have a classmate time you. Then assess the fluency and legibility of your writing.

Date __/__/__ Time taken: __ seconds

A black, hazy cloud just quietly wafted from the gaping mouth of the extinct volcano!

Rate your fluency.

Rate your legibility.

Date __/__/__ Time taken: __ seconds

A black, hazy cloud just quietly wafted from the gaping mouth of the extinct volcano!

Rate your fluency.

Rate your legibility.

Date ___/___/___ Time taken: ___ seconds

A black, hazy cloud just quietly wafted from the gaping mouth of the extinct volcano!

Rate your fluency.

Rate your legibility.

Date ___/___/___ Time taken: ___ seconds

A black, hazy cloud just quietly wafted from the gaping mouth of the extinct volcano!

Rate your fluency.

Rate your legibility.

Date ___/___/___ Time taken: ___ seconds

A black, hazy cloud just quietly wafted from the gaping mouth of the extinct volcano!

Rate your fluency.

Rate your legibility.

Date ___/___/___

Copy.

a b c d e f g h i j k l m

n o p q r s t u v w x y z

The quick brown fox jumps over

the head of the lazy dog.

Copy.

A B C D E F G H I J K L M

N O P Q R S T U V W X Y Z

1 2 3 4 5 6 7 8 9 10 20 30 40 50

Date __/__/__

Trace, then copy.

am ap ce cr di er he is

ks ly me pr sp ti un xe

deep limp ninny mixer quiz

Natural disasters like volcanoes

and earthquakes affect the shape of

the world we live in.

SELF ASSESSMENT

Rate your diagonal joins.

Needs work Force 5 Earth-shaking!

Date ___/___/___

When joining from s, retrace the bottom of the s before you go on to join.

sn
retrace

Trace, then copy.

sp sw st sy se si sm su sn

reason super swiftly easy

answer reverse resist spine

On 26 December 2003, an earthquake destroyed the city of Bam, Iran, leaving at least 70 000 homeless.

SELF ASSESSMENT

Circle your three best diagonal joins from s.

Date __/__/__
Revision – Horizontal joins
Use a horizontal join when joining from b, o, r, v, and w. These horizontal joins have a small dip.
small dip
ru vi or
Horizontal joins from f join from the crossbar.
fi fr
IDRS
Trace, then copy.
bi br bu op or ow ri rn
ro rv vi wi wn wr fi fr
bin loud avid own storm
furry frill fitness fringe
Thunderstorms can be loud!
SELF ASSESSMENT
Rate your horizontal joins.
Needs work
Force 5
Earth-shaking!

☆ Revision – Horizontal joins to e

Date ___/___/___

Trace, then copy.

be re ve we fe re we

best canoe feature active

relaxed some poetry velvet

Tornadoes are very powerful and

can wreck heavy vehicles.

SELF ASSESSMENT

Underline your best three best horizontal joins to e.

Date __/__/__

Trace, then copy. For the first line, put a star ✳ to show each place where you lifted your pen.

ac pa dg eq sa eg ma nd

ig ed ng da iq nc xa ta

equal half piglet tangy

Avalanches can occur after an

earthquake dislodges loose snow.

SELF ASSESSMENT

Rate your touch joins.

Needs work Force 5 Earth-shaking!

Date ___/___/___

Trace, then copy.

ba oc rg rd va wa rq fa

road word wasted vamoose

fair torque rock batch

Lava is liquid rock that erupts

from a volcano.

SELF ASSESSMENT

Circle your three best touch joins.

Date ___/___/___

When joining horizontally to s, go right across the top of the s, then retrace the top before heading down.

When joining to s with a diagonal join, make the top of the s shorter.

os retrace fs retrace

ls top shorter as

Trace, then copy.

os rs ws fs ns is ts es

post verse ribs reefs bowser

blizzards typhoons avalanches

Most firestorms can hurl flaming debris for kilometres.

SELF ASSESSMENT

Rate your joins to s.

Needs work

Force 5

Earth-shaking!

☆ Revision – Joining to o and from o

Date __/__/__

When making a diagonal or horizontal join to the letter o, go right across to o's starting point then retrace a little before you head back down.

Remember to retrace when joining after o. Do not make a loop.

retrace no retrace wo retrace on don't loop! on

Trace, then copy.

bo wo oo mo co oi on ot

wood tomorrow oboe love

On 31 December 2004, an avalanche stuck Mt Tasman, New Zealand, and knocked a group of climbers 300 metres down the mountain.

SELF ASSESSMENT

Circle your best join to o and your best join from o.

Date __/__/__

Trace, then copy.

af ef lf if uf of rf wf

reef chef elf hoof surf

fa fe fi fo fu fl fr

fake feat fit after before

SELF ASSESSMENT

Rate your joins **to** f.

Needs work Force 5 Earth-shaking!

☆ Revision – Joining to f and from f

Date __/__/__

Remember – f at the beginning of a word doesn't have a loop.

Trace, then copy.

fire fair fend food fret

thief turf roof half shelf

raft sift softly life leafy

One after-effect of a fire is often a season of rapid regrowth.

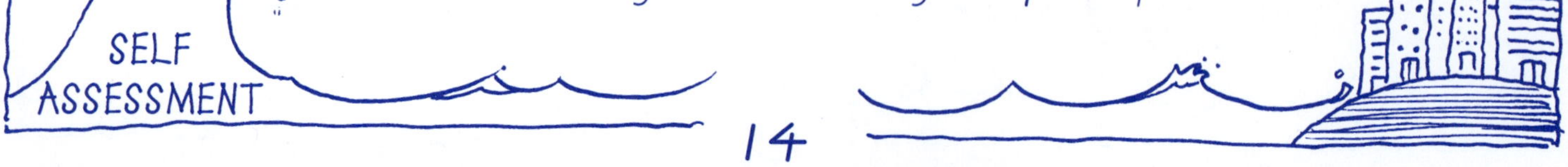

SELF ASSESSMENT

Circle your three best joins **from** f.

Date __/__/__

traffic muffle

Trace, then copy.

ff ff ff ff ff ff ff ff

puff diff scuffle effective

affirm different fluffy truffle

In 1977, Buffalo, New York, was

buffeted by a huge blizzard.

SELF ASSESSMENT

Rate your joined double f's.

Date __/__/__

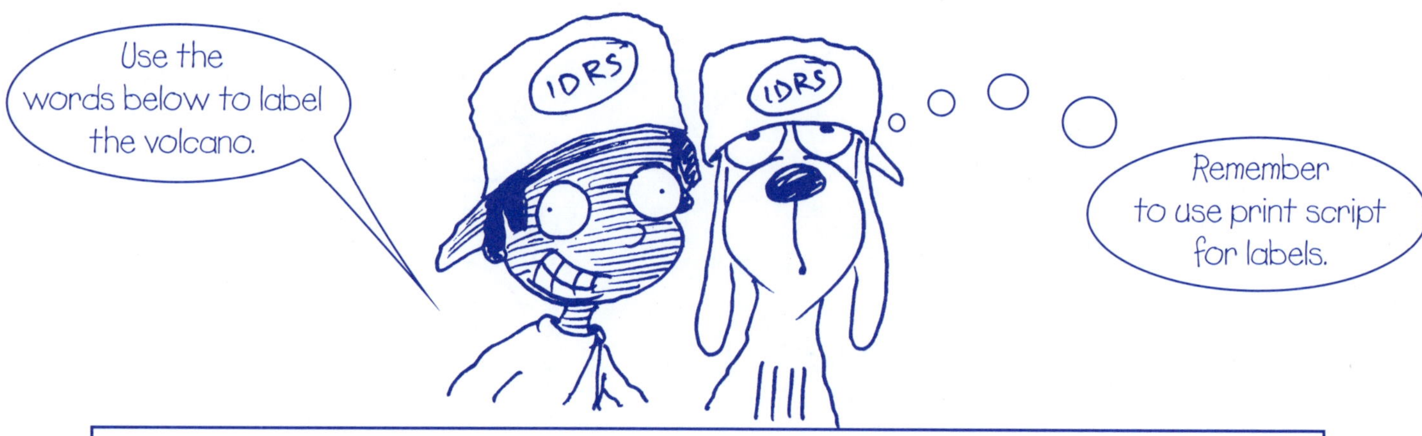

main vent	cone	ash cloud
side vent	lava	magma chamber

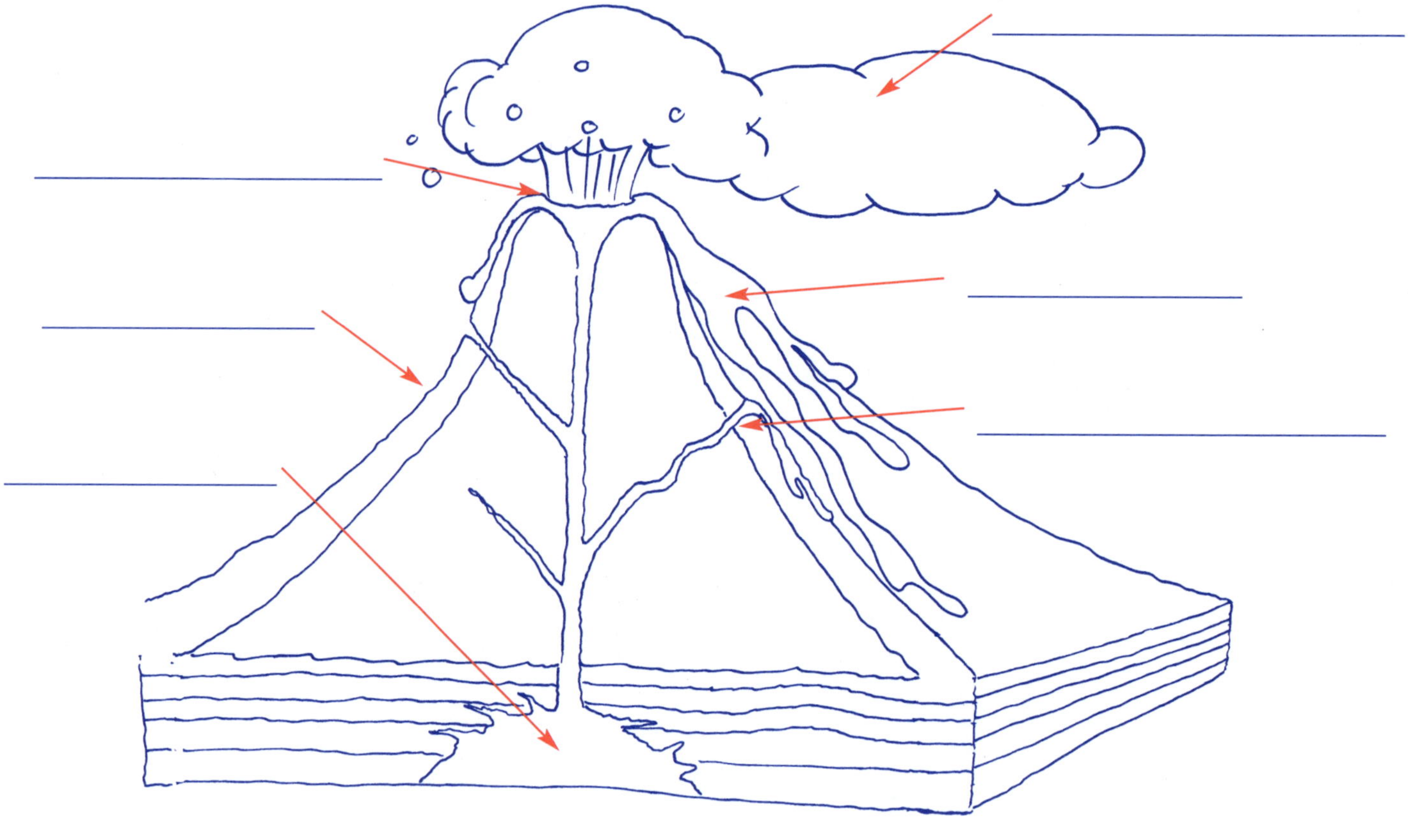

Rewrite this sentence in print script.

When Krakatau Volcano erupted in 1883, people more than 4800 kilometres away heard the roar.

Date __/__/__

Write each word in joined writing.

Diagonal joins

minty element ukulele think

Horizontal joins

boiling burp weasel heroes

Touch joins

trace aqua bandage icicle

Joining to s and from s; joining to o and from o

rosy eraser robot pillows

Joining to f and from f

turf fret safer puffy

Teacher

Date ___/___/___

Speed loops can help you write more fluently when joining from g, j, y and z.

Speed loops from body and tail letters should cross at the baseline.

glad jump yes

speed loop crosses at baseline

Trace, then copy.

g g ga ge gift gone gap

j j ja je jig jet just

y y ya ye yes yip yarn

z z zi zo zip zone zap

Go easy in the danger zone!

SELF ASSESSMENT

Circle your best speed loops from g, j, y and z.

Date ___/___/___

Speed loops mean you don't always have to slow down to retrace carefully.

Speed loops to head and body letters should cross at the magic line.

speed loop crosses at magic line

real each

Trace, then copy.

l l al el il ol ul ll

pearl ally plain glad

h h oh ch gh ph sh th

child laugh graph shine

Howling blizzards are chilly!

SELF ASSESSMENT

Rate your speed loops to l and h.

Needs work Force 5 Earth-shaking!

Revision – Speed loops to b and k

Date ___/___/___

Don't make your speed loops too big, or they will slow you down!

✓ climb NOT climb ✗

Trace, then copy.

b b ab eb ib ob ub obb

able rebel tribe robe bulb

k k ak ck lk nk rk sk

risk talk knack work

Twisters look like big trouble!

SELF ASSESSMENT

Circle the words that have your best speed loops to b and k.

Date ___/___/___

Trace, then copy.

rd de ot tr sp pi sq qu

muddle skittle sipping speed

would aquarium little later

Two children buried under the rubble of a powerful earthquake attracted attention by singing.

SELF ASSESSMENT

Rate your joined writing.

Needs work Force 5 Earth-shaking!

Date __/__/__

Head and body letters don't have a speed loop at the beginning of a word, because the letter has not joined from anything.

no speed loop

✓ land NOT land ✗

It's OK to loop from a body and tail letter at the end of a word.

holiday

Trace, then copy.

A man went on a holiday and

forgot to turn off his lawn

sprinkler. All the water made his

house slide down the mountain!

SELF ASSESSMENT

Circle the three words that have your best speed loops.

Date __/__/__

Copy, adding speed loops to the letters that need them.

angry gecko just jelly

royal zebra oboe bully

desk think hoax luck

Rewrite this passage in cursive script, using speed loops.

In 1999, 4 alligators survived a fire in an aquarium in the U.S. The owner kept them briefly in his bathtub at home.

Teacher

Date ___/___/___

Now you can write smaller. The space between the blue lines can be divided into three sections. The letter bodies sit on the blue line in the bottom third, and the letter heads sit in the middle third.

The top third allows space for the tails of letters from the line above.

Top third
Middle third
Bottom third

Disaster fighters
wanted

Top third
Middle third
Bottom third

Copy, using the red lines to help with letter sizing.

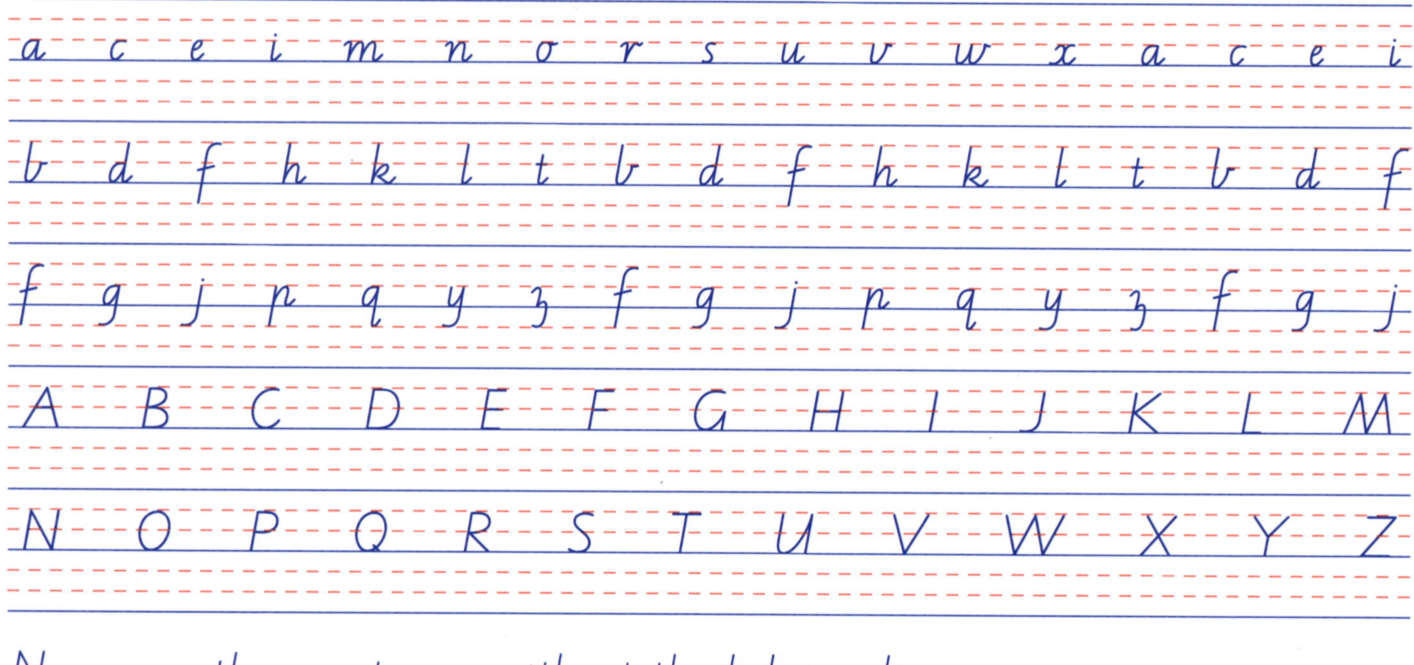

Now copy these sentences without the helping lines.

In January and February 2003, lightning strikes caused uncontrollable bushfires in north-eastern Victoria. The fires raged for over 42 days.

SELF ASSESSMENT

Rate your writing on 8 mm lines.

Needs work *Force 5* *Earth-shaking!*

Date __/__/__

nose waver reams miner verse minimum

little kitten filter kilt bidden handed

grange jumpy gypsy quip jeep guppy

The worst hail disaster occurred in a place called Moradabad, India, in 1888. The hailstones were the size of cricket balls, and 246 people died.

Date __/__/__

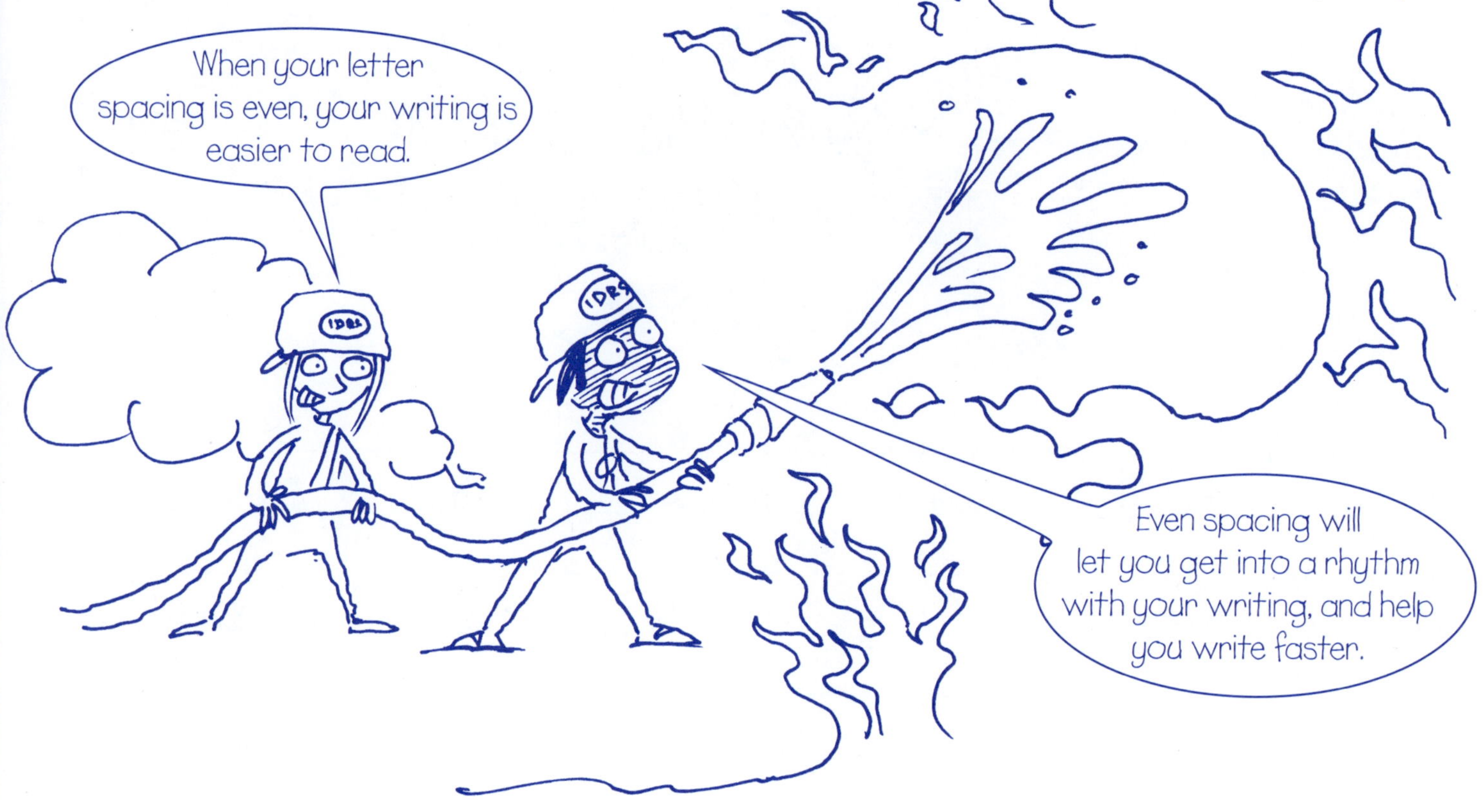

When your letter spacing is even, your writing is easier to read.
IDRS
IDRS
Even spacing will let you get into a rhythm with your writing, and help you write faster.

firestorm NOT *fi rest orm*

Copy the following passage, aiming to keep your letter spacing even.

A huge fire started in Washington, U.S. on 6 August 2000. Investigators were called in to find out what had caused it. The fire had begun when a grasshopper struck an electric fence, caught fire and fell into tall, dry grass.

SELF ASSESSMENT

Circle the three words with the most even letter spacing.

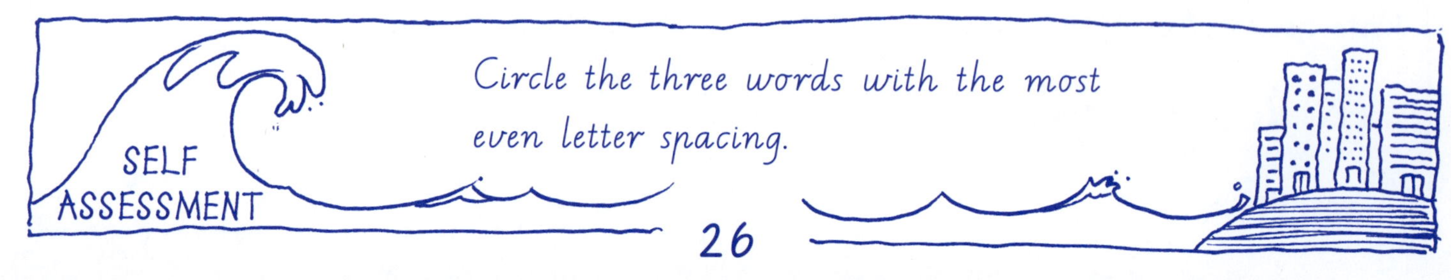

Date __/__/__

element — even letter spacing

el eme nt — uneven letter spacing

Copy, then choose one line and use dots to check your spacing.

As the Earth moves through space, pieces of debris enter its atmosphere. Most vaporise straight away — you see them at night as shooting stars. However, the meteor that exploded over Tunguska, Siberia in 1908 was much bigger. The explosion flattened trees over an area 50 kilometres wide and shot flames 20 kilometres into the air.

SELF ASSESSMENT

Rate your letter spacing.

Needs work — Force 5 — Earth-shaking!

Date __/__/__

When you space your words out evenly, your writing is much easier to read.

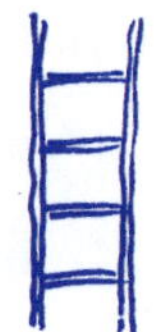

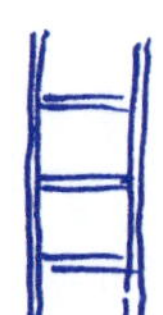

Copy out the following passage, aiming to keep your word spacing even.

On 22 February 1845, a day after leaving Mauritius,

a ship called the "Charles Heddles" ran into an

enormous storm. The captain ran the ship before the

wind for a whole week. When the weather calmed,

the ship was only a few kilometres off Mauritius!

It had been going in circles for that whole week,

caught in a cyclone.

SELF ASSESSMENT

Tick the line that has the most even word spacing.

Tornadoes o are o sometimes o called o twisters.

Tornadoes are sometimes called twisters. o's won't fit between words

Tornadoes o are o sometimes o called o twisters. too spacy

In a tornado in Indiana, U.S. in 1974, a house was demolished. The only thing that survived was the kitchen cupboard, which was carried away. The cupboard later settled back to Earth with every dish intact.

SELF ASSESSMENT

Rate your word spacing.

Needs work Force 5 Earth-shaking!

Date __/__/__

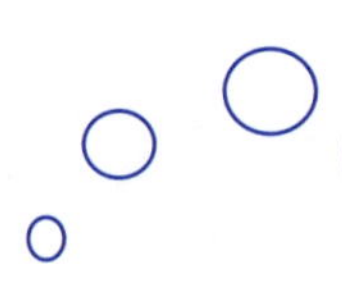

Your writing will be easier to read if all the letters slope in the same direction, and the same amount.

Before you copy the text below, check your posture, paper position and pencil grip. Getting these things right first will make it easier to keep your slope even.

Copy the passage, aiming to keep the slope of your letters consistent.

A device called a creepmeter can be used to alert people to earthquake danger. The creepmeter is buried in the ground. It is attached to sensors that are placed close to a faultline. The sensors measure tiny movements that can give warning of an earthquake.

Tick the line in which your slope is the most consistent.

Date __/__/__

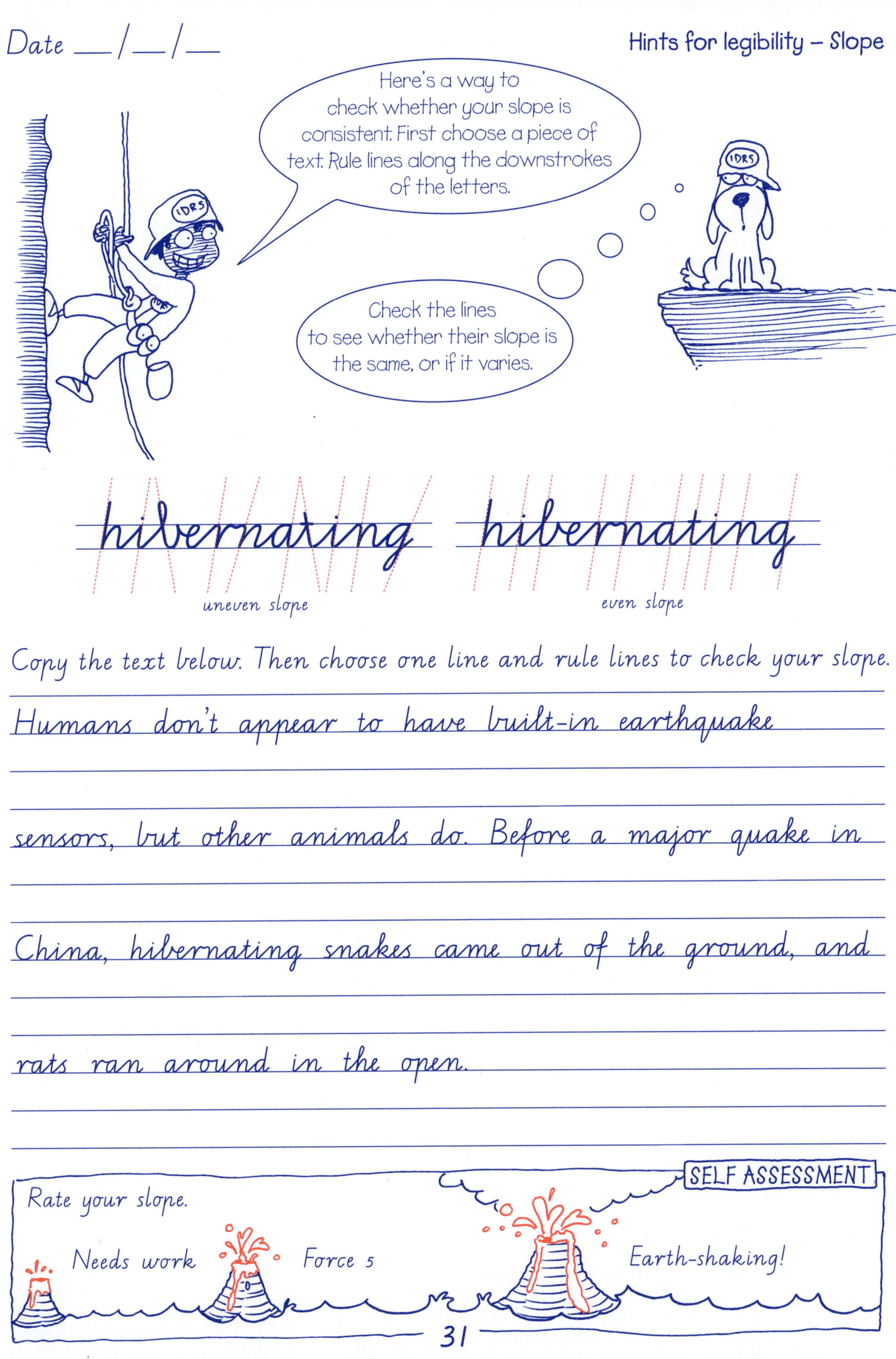

Copy the text below. Then choose one line and rule lines to check your slope.

Humans don't appear to have built-in earthquake
sensors, but other animals do. Before a major quake in
China, hibernating snakes came out of the ground, and
rats ran around in the open.

Date ___/___/___

Copy. Make a dot at each place where your writing touches the baseline to check your letter spacing. Rule a line along the top of the letter bodies to check if they are the same size.

There was a major earthquake in Mexico City in 1985.

Copy. Write an o between each word to check your word spacing. Rule a line across the top of the letter heads to see if they are the same height.

People who were left homeless set up makeshift camps made of plastic, blankets, and pieces of furniture.

Copy, then choose one line. Rule lines along the downstrokes to check your slope. Then rule a line across the bottom of the letter tails to see if they are the same length.

Someone managed to set up a TV. There was no food or water, but there was televised soccer!

Date __/__/__

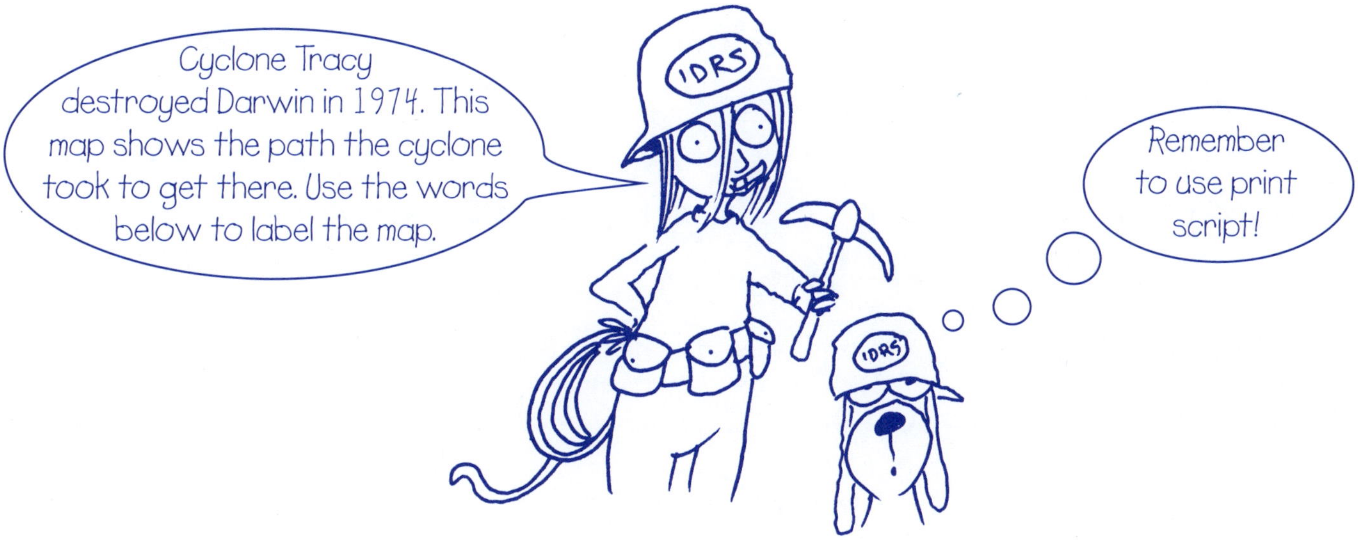

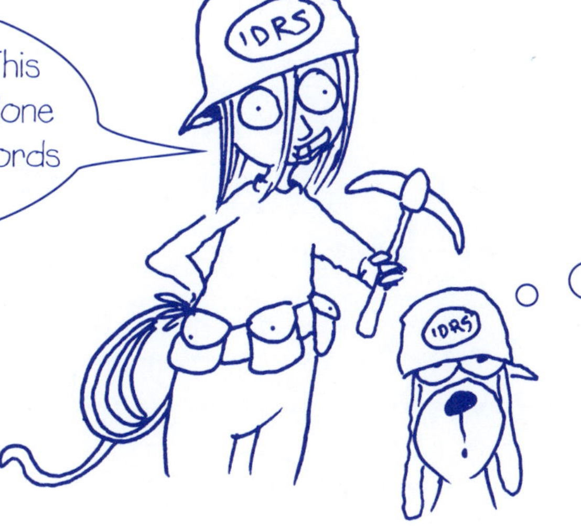

TIMOR SEA   *Melville Island*   ARAFURA SEA

Path of storm   NORTHERN TERRITORY   *Darwin*

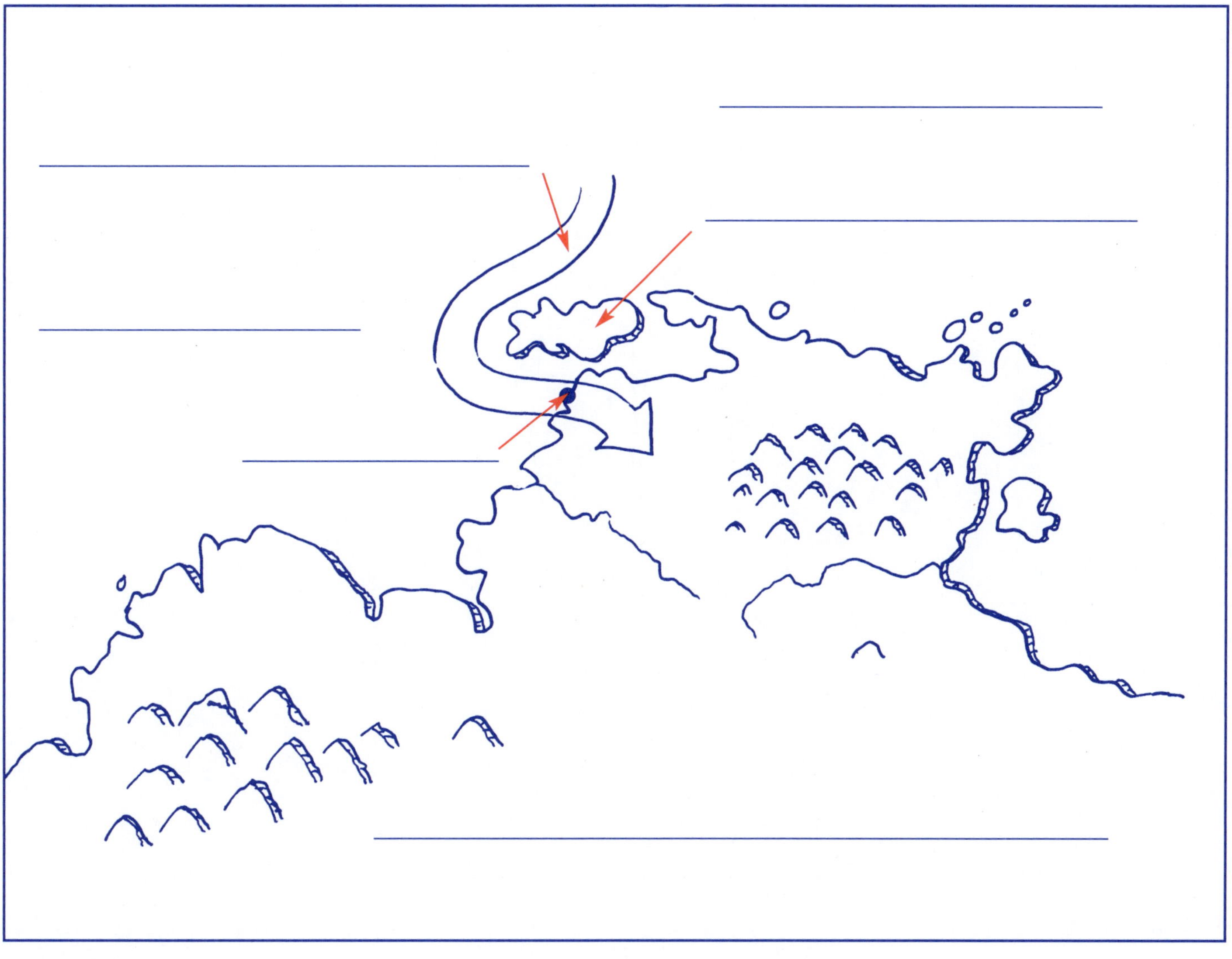

Date ___/___/___

For interstellar rescues, you need a spacesuit! Label this diagram using print script. Then write out the list of components in cursive.

Gloves	Boots	Visor	Chest-mounted control module
Pocket	Life-support backpack	Helmet	
Communication, oxygen and cooling connectors			

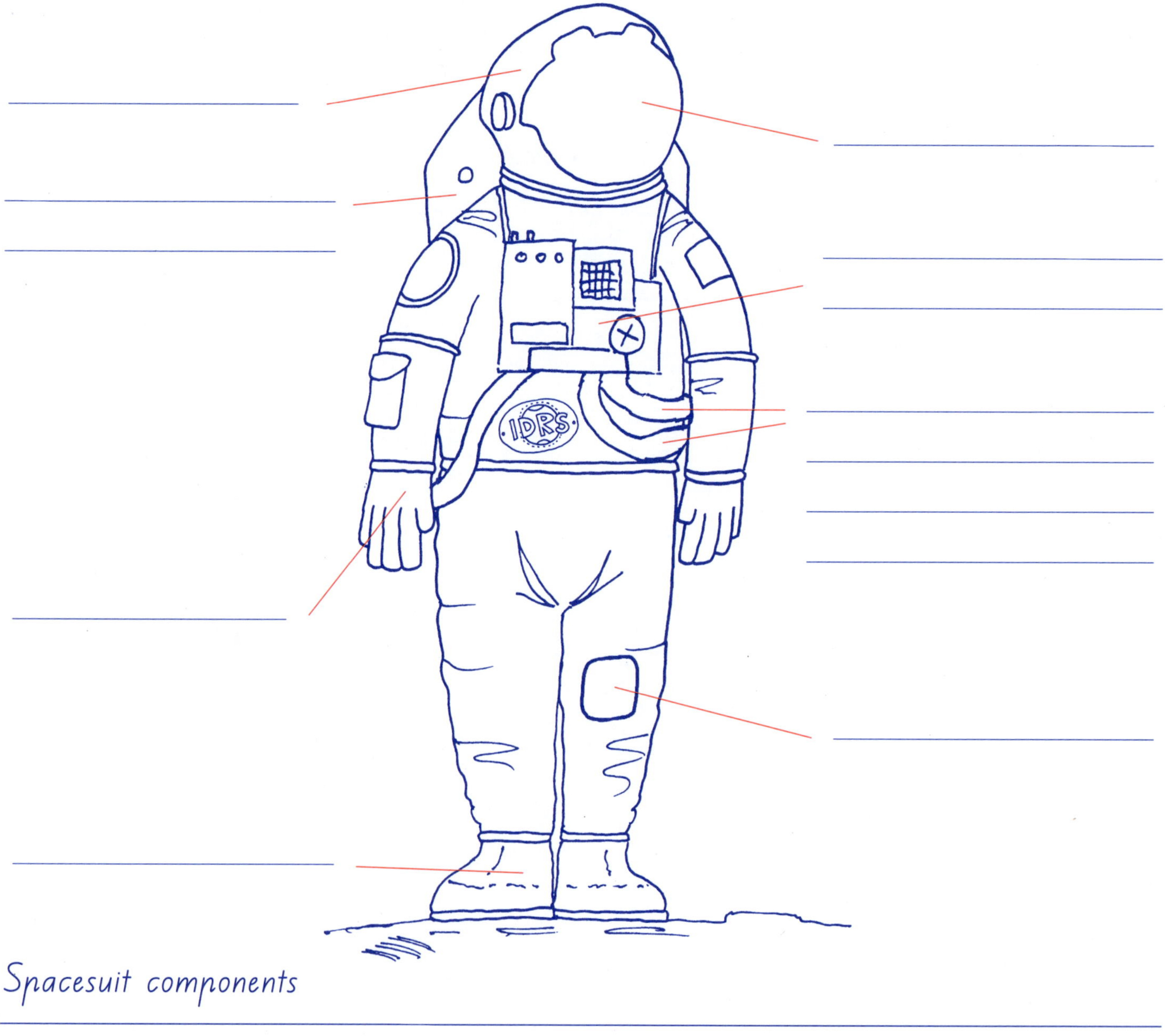

Spacesuit components

Date ___/___/___

Intensity Phrase

Gale tornado, Moderate tornado, Significant tornado, Severe tornado, Devastating tornado, Incredible tornado

Type of Damage Done

F_0 chimney and sign damage, tree branches broken
F_1 caravans overturned, cars pushed off roads
F_2 roofs torn off weaker buildings, trees uprooted
F_3 roofs and walls torn down, trains overturned
F_4 well-constructed houses flattened
F_5 homes lifted and carried considerable distances

The Fujita-Pearson Tornado Scale

F-Scale Number	Intensity Phrase	Wind Speed (km/h)	Type of Damage Done
F_0		64–116	
F_1		117–180	
F_2		181–253	
F_3		254–332	
F_4		333–419	
F_5		420–512	

Date __/__/__

Do a class survey to find out how many people have experienced these natural events.

Tally your results in the table below. Use these headings: Hailstorm, Thunderstorm, Flood, Fire, Drought, Earthquake, Cyclone, Avalanche, Volcanic Eruption. Write them in print script.

Graph your results. Use print script for the labels and heading of your graph.

Date __/__/__

Write the alphabet in print script.

Rewrite this list of live volcanoes in print script.

Etna, Italy	
Santa Maria, Guatemala	
Lamongon, Indonesia	
Mount Oyama, Japan	
Rabaul, Papua New Guinea	
Krakatau, Indonesia	
San Cristobal, Nicaragua	
Pinatubo, Philippines	
Mauna Loa, Hawaii	
Rotorua, New Zealand	
Arenal, Costa Rica	
Karymsky, Russia	
Kilauea, Hawaii	
Shishaldin, Alaska	
Grimsvotn, Iceland	
Lascar, Chile	
Reventador, Ecuador	

Date ___/___/___

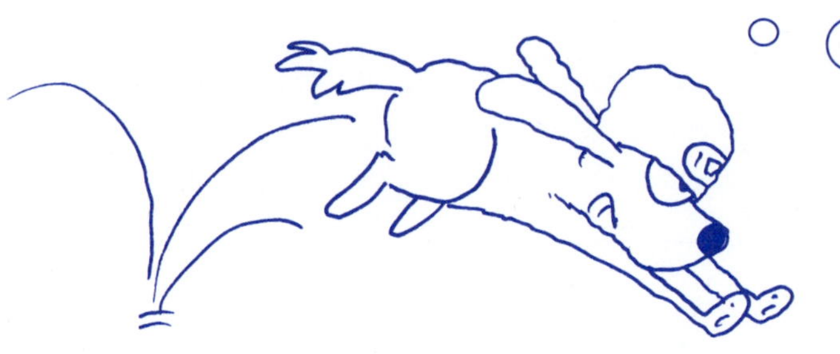

Make your diagonal joins go directly to the next letter. This will make your writing faster and easier to read.

hunt brittle climb amulet drizzle splint

Tropical cyclones are also known as hurricanes or

typhoons. From 80 to 100 cyclones develop over tropical

oceans each year. These are the biggest and strongest

storms. Most are more than 200 km wide. At the

centre is a calm area called the eye. Near the eye,

wind speeds can be greater than 300 km/h.

SELF ASSESSMENT

Circle your three best diagonal joins.
Tick the line with the best letter spacing.

Horizontal joins have a small dip, except for horizontal joins from f. The letter f joins from the crossbar.

Remember, the crossbar is lower when you join from f to e.

Bombs, or blocks, are chunks of half-solid, half-molten lava that shoot out of a volcano. The four different kinds of bombs have names that depend on their shape — for example, there is a kind of bomb known as "cow dung". A bomb can be as big as a house, or as small as a tennis ball.

SELF ASSESSMENT

Rate your horizontal joins.

☆ ☆☆ ☆☆☆

Rate your letter spacing.

☆ ☆☆ ☆☆☆

Date ___/___/___

bigger dip

we

echoed cover renew weevil amber vent

mangoes alive weather beast rear venom

If you are outside during an earthquake, move away

from tall buildings or other structures, overhead

power lines, elevated freeways, or anything that could

fall on you. Lie down, or crouch, and cover your

head. Beware of flying glass or falling objects.

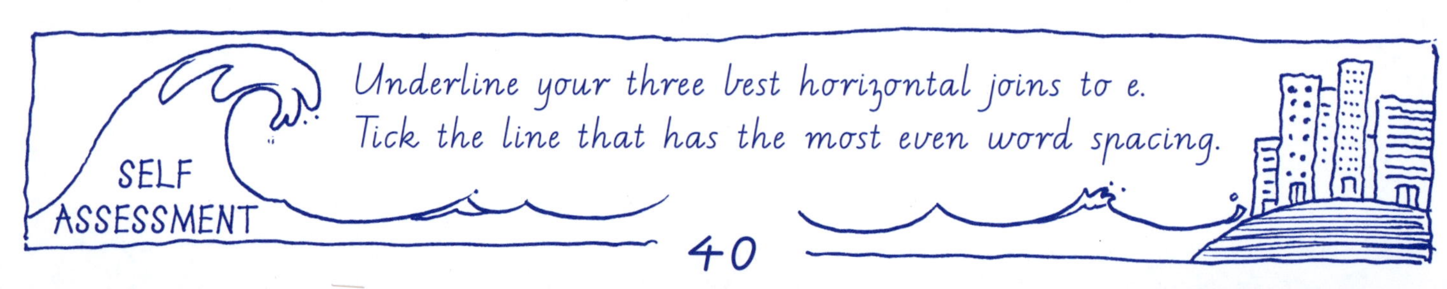

Underline your three best horizontal joins to e.
Tick the line that has the most even word spacing.

Date ___/___/___

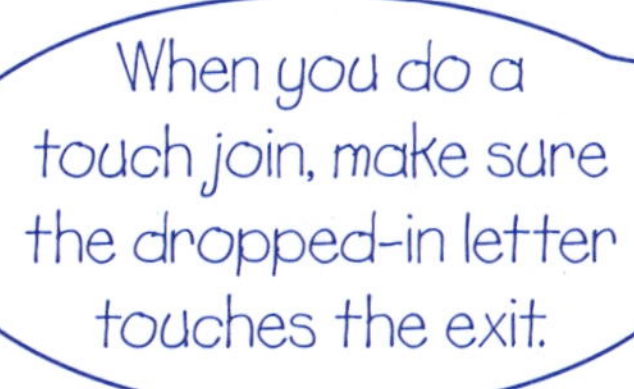

late ogre idea hoard specific equator

Cyclone Tracy, a small but intense tropical cyclone,
hit Darwin on Christmas Day in 1974. The winds
reached speeds over 240 km/h. The city was almost
completely destroyed, and 65 people were killed — 49
on land and 16 at sea. Afterwards, in many suburbs
of Darwin only the telegraph poles were left standing.

SELF ASSESSMENT

Rate your touch joins.

☆ ☆☆ ☆☆☆

Rate your word spacing.

☆ ☆☆ ☆☆☆

Date ___/___/___

second s is shorter at the top

the two s's are the same

toss messy

horizontal join

diagonal join

boss toss across glossy gossip possum

pass glassy less message hiss missile

When water blows through liquid lava, the lava can cool into glossy strands of glass called "Pele's hair". Pele is the Hawaiian volcano goddess. One strand can be 0.5 mm wide but 2 m long.

SELF ASSESSMENT

Circle your three best double s's.
Tick the line with the best slope.

Date __/__/__

Draw lines to match the double letters with the error that has been made.

rr	loops instead of retracing
ee	uneven size of speed loops
oo	no exit on first letter
ll	letters spaced too far apart
tt	uneven letter size
nn	inconsistent slope
mm	crossbar not level

Copy.

rr rr ee oo oo ll tt tt nn mm

hurricane terror need creep typhoon monsoon

spelling hollow shrill pattern butter thinner

connect simmer mammal drummed balloon

SELF ASSESSMENT

Rate your double letters. ☆ ☆☆ ☆☆☆

Rate your slope. ☆ ☆☆ ☆☆☆

Date __/__/__

Try making your downstrokes firm and your upstrokes lighter. This will give you a feel for the rhythm of your writing.

Every year about sixty volcanoes erupt around the world. Some volcanoes stay dormant for hundreds of years before they erupt again. Other volcanoes — like Stromboli Volcano in Italy — erupt regularly. Stromboli has been erupting about every 20 minutes for more than 2 500 years. Sailors call it the Lighthouse of the Mediterranean because you can see the volcano's ashes glowing from out at sea.

SELF ASSESSMENT

Tick the line that has the best speed loops.

Date __/__/__

Assessment page – Fluency and legibility

Write these words and sentences in joined writing.

slime kettle minty enter slither element

view west bent roof filter bite refer

yelled waif claim etiquette racer reading

fades lesser monsters reefs crossing arrows

skiff baffle punnet moon silly putty

gypsy junior hitch ballast streak double

There was a magnitude 6.9 earthquake in north-western Armenia on 7 December 1988. Buildings crumbled, roads cracked and bridges collapsed. Whole cities and villages were destroyed and many people were killed. Afterwards a carton of eggs was spotted in the rubble. Not one egg had broken.

Teacher

Date ___/___/___

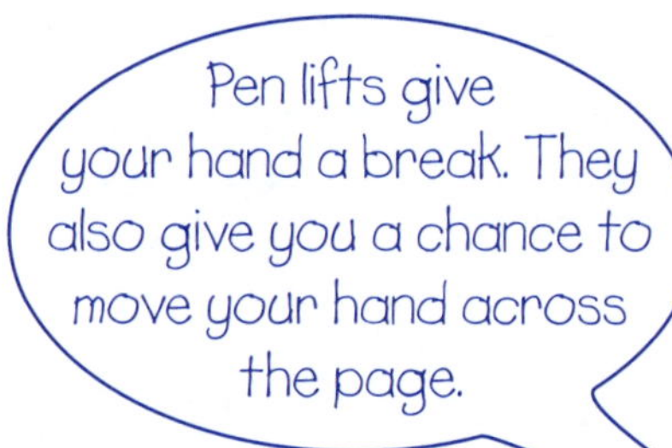

Choose one line and make a mark like this ' above each place you will lift your pencil. Copy.

Francis Beaufort was a Commander in the Royal

Navy. In 1806, he invented a scale to estimate wind

speeds. At Force 0 (calm), smoke rises vertically.

At Force 5 (a fresh breeze), small trees sway.

At Force 9 (a strong gale), slate is blown from roofs.

A Force 12 storm causes widespread destruction.

Date ___/___/___

The intensity of an earthquake can be rated using the Modified Mercalli Scale. The scale is divided into 12 parts, and each is given a Roman numeral. At intensity I, instruments can detect the earthquake, but people don't feel it. At VI, pictures fall off walls and furniture moves. At intensity IX, houses that aren't bolted down move off their foundations. At intensity XII, almost everything is destroyed.

Date ___/___/___

Make a mark like this ′ above each place you had to lift your pen that was **not** a touch join.

telecommunication elementary scholarship

biographical celebration challenging

characteristic circumstance demonstration

determination encouragement environmental

fluorescent forbidding headquarters

High temperatures can cause uncontrollable blazes.

Circle your best long word.

Copy these tips for safety in the event of a fire.

- Crawl low through smoke.

- Before you open a door in a fire, feel it. If it's hot, don't open it!

- Get out and stay out. NEVER go back for possessions.

- If anyone is still inside, tell an adult.

SELF ASSESSMENT

Rate your letter spacing.

☆ ☆ ☆ ☆ ☆ ☆

Rate your word spacing.

☆ ☆ ☆ ☆ ☆ ☆

Date __/__/__

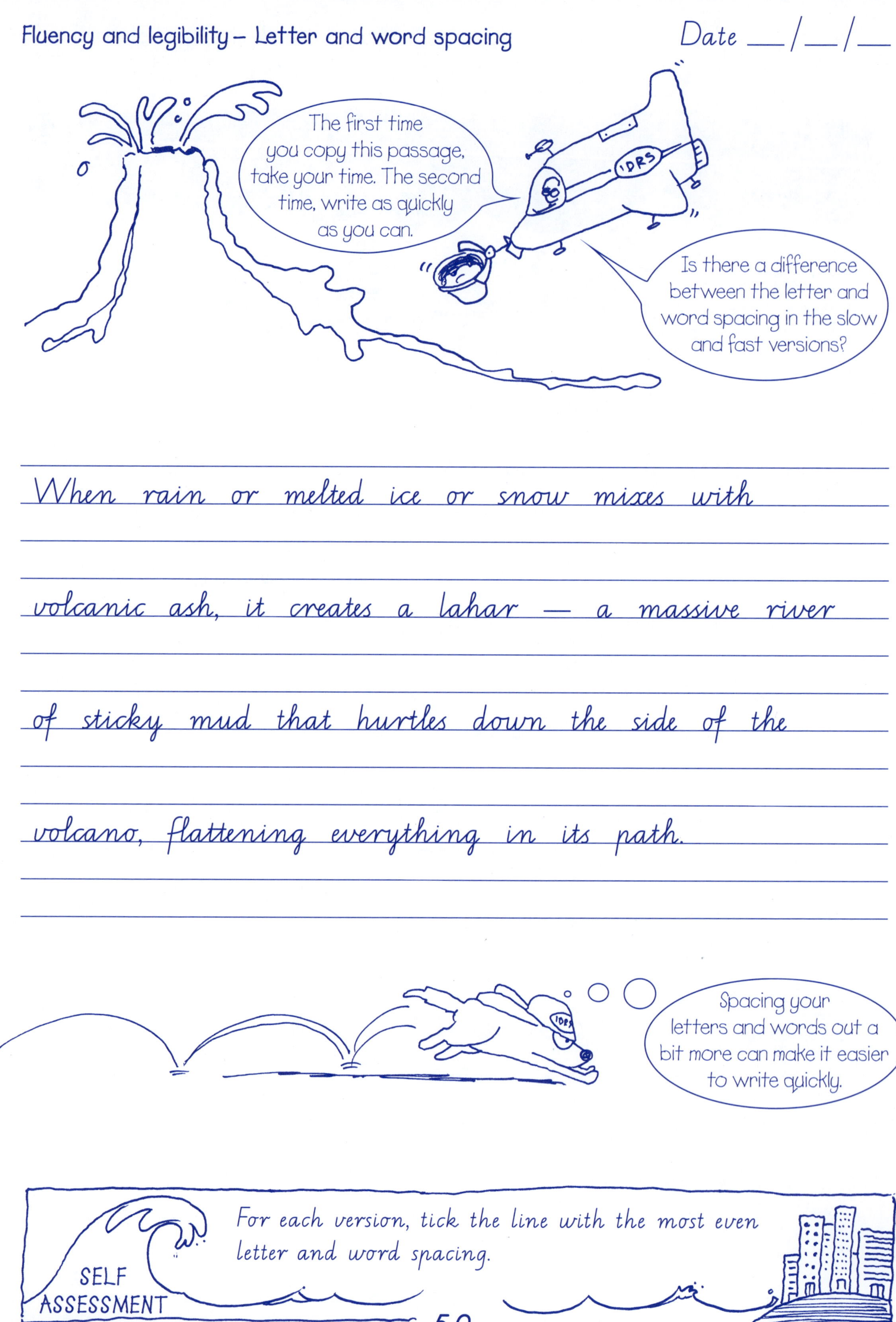
The first time you copy this passage, take your time. The second time, write as quickly as you can.
Is there a difference between the letter and word spacing in the slow and fast versions?
IDRS
When rain or melted ice or snow mixes with
volcanic ash, it creates a lahar — a massive river
of sticky mud that hurtles down the side of the
volcano, flattening everything in its path.
Spacing your letters and words out a bit more can make it easier to write quickly.
SELF ASSESSMENT
For each version, tick the line with the most even letter and word spacing.

Heavy snowfalls deposit large unstable masses of snow

on steep slopes. This increases the risk of avalanches.

An avalanche can be triggered by a movement, a

gust of wind or a loud noise.

SELF ASSESSMENT

Rate slope when writing slowly. ☆ ☆☆ ☆☆☆

Rate your slope when writing quickly. ☆ ☆☆ ☆☆☆

Date __/__/__

Fill in this disaster report, using capitals only.

International Disaster Rescue Squad Report

NATURE OF DISASTER: ____________________________

____

WHERE: ____

____

WHEN (DATE AND TIME): __________________________

____

CASUALTIES: ____________________________________

____

STEPS TAKEN TO HELP: ___________________________

____

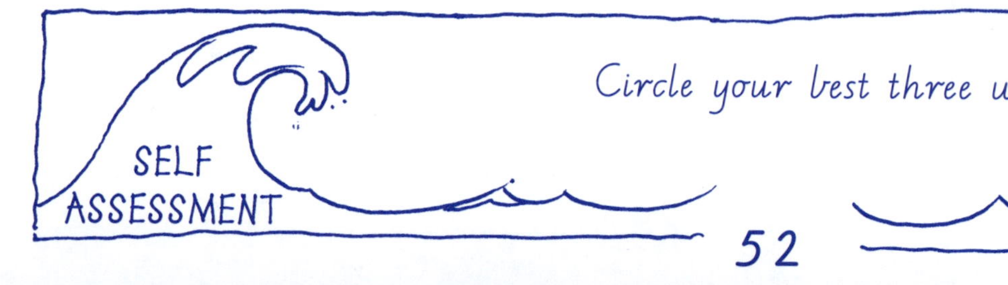

Circle your best three words.

Date __/__/__

Copy out the jokes below, making sure you include all the punctuation.

Q. What did one mountain say to the other mountain after the earthquake?
A. "It's not my fault!"

Q. What happens to cows after earthquakes?
A. They give milkshakes.

Q. What is a volcano?
A. A mountain with hiccups.

SELF ASSESSMENT

Rate your punctuation.
☆ ☆☆ ☆☆☆

Rate your word spacing.
☆ ☆☆ ☆☆☆

Date ___/___/___

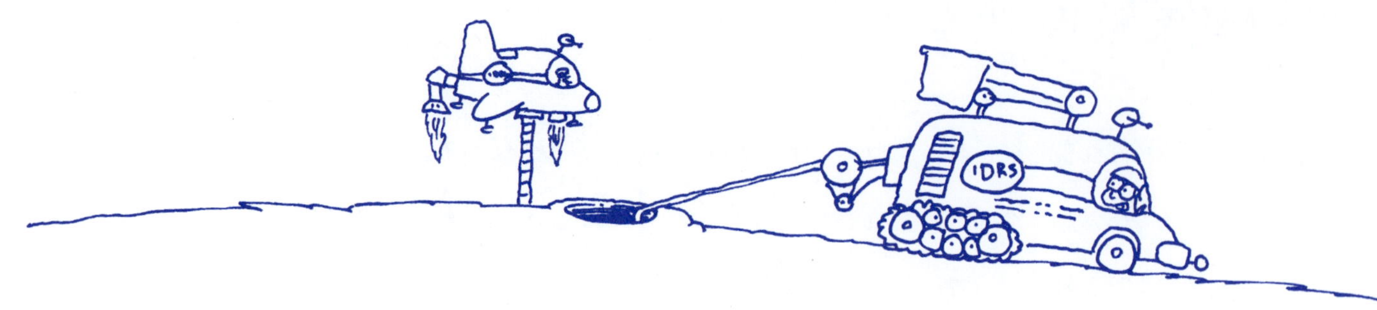

Copy these letter clusters and words.

scr scr scr scrap scrub scribble scratch

ght ght ght night flight weight laughter

spl spl spl split spleen splinter splendid

dge dge dge dodgy nudge fridge wedge

squ squ squ squeal squall squishy squash

nce nce nce prince mince advance dancer

SELF ASSESSMENT

Tick the line with the most consistent letter spacing.

Date __/__/__

Copy these letter clusters and words.

spr spr spr spring spread spry sprung

nch nch nch lunch winch inch stench

str str str strong stripe street string

gle gle gle giggle wriggle jungle muggle

tch tch tch watch itchy scratch blotch

Write a short sentence that includes two of these letter clusters.

SELF ASSESSMENT

Rate your touch joins. ☆ ☆☆ ☆☆☆

Rate your slope. ☆ ☆☆ ☆☆☆

Date ___/___/___

This page will give you practice in words you have to write a lot.

of an it at if is or he be to

the and who are you not has for

she was you with this have when

will more they were said there which

Write a sentence, including as many of these words as you can.

SELF ASSESSMENT

Circle three words with good letter spacing.

Date __/__/__

Copy the following passage. Then:

- ★ choose one line and add a dot at each point where your writing touches the baseline
- ★ choose another line and write an o between each word
- ★ choose another line and rule lines along the downstrokes.

Volcanoes are not just found on Earth. In
1979, two Voyager spacecraft flew past Jupiter's
moon Io and sent back pictures. Eight
volcanoes could be seen erupting! In March
1995, astronomers who were looking at Io
through a telescope saw a massive eruption.

Teacher

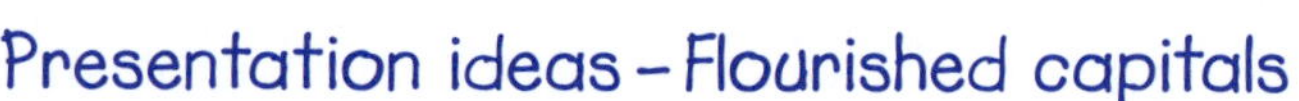

Presentation ideas – Flourished capitals

Trace then copy the flourished capitals.

A A A A A A

B B B B B B

C C C C C C

D D D D D D

E E E E E E

F F F F F F

G G G G G G

H H H H H H

I I I I I I

J J J J J J

SELF ASSESSMENT

Circle your best example of each flourished capital.

Date ___/___/___

K K K K K K

L L L L L L

M M M M M M

N N N N N N

O O O O O O

P P P P P P

Q Q Q Q Q Q

R R R R R R

S S S S S S

T T T T T T

U U U U U U

V V V V V V

W W W W W W

X X X X X X

Y Y Y Y Y Y

Z Z Z Z Z Z

Now practise writing flourished capitals.

A B C D E F G H I J K L M

N O P Q R S T U V W X Y Z

SELF ASSESSMENT

Circle your best example of each flourished capital.

Date ___/___/___

Antigua Bahamas Chile Darwin Ecuador

Florida Guadeloupe Himalayas Iceland

Jamaica Kobe Lisbon Mexico Netherlands

Osaka Philippines Quebec Russia

Sumatra Turkey United States Vancouver

West Indies Xinhua Yugoslavia Zeeland

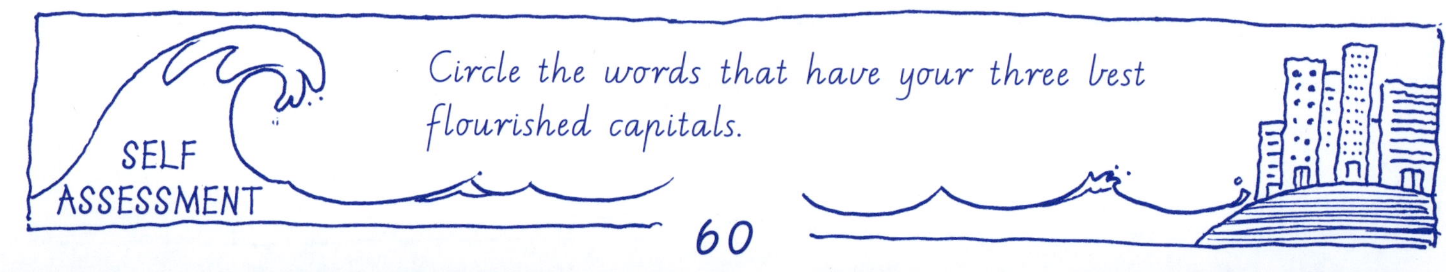

Date __/__/__

The Top Five Deadliest Earthquakes in History

Where	When	Deaths
Shaunxi, China	1556	830,000
Calcutta, India	1737	300,000
Tangshan, China	1976	255,000
Aleppo, Syria	1138	230,000
Near Xining, China	1927	200,000

SELF ASSESSMENT

Rate your flourished capitals.

Needs work — Force 5 — Earth-shaking!

Date ___/___/___

An Al Be Cr Cl Em Fr Ga

Hi Ha In Ir Ke Kh La Mo

Ma Re Ri Un Ul Xe Ze Za

Alison Boris Clint Evie Irfan

Monday Easter April Swan Hill

Try some joined flourished capitals of your own. Make sure each capital letter's shape is still clear.

Date __/__/__
Presentation ideas – Headings
TSUNAMI
IDRS
This is a word picture. Words pictures can make great headings. Try making your own, using some of the words below.
Earthquake
Landslide
Avalanche
Firestorm
Volcano
Tornado

Date ___/___/___

On another piece of paper, write about your most exciting day as a member of the International Disaster Rescue Squad. Copy the final draft onto this page in your best cursive writing. Add a heading and an appropriate border.